A SUMMER OUTSIDE

Looking inside

Christiaan van Gaal

Photobook & short poems

Only a Fool! Only a Poet!

When the air grows clear,
when the dew's comfort already
rains down upon the earth,
invisible and unheard
- for dew the comforter
wears tender shoes like all that gently comforts -
do you then remember, do you, hot heart,
how once you thirsted
for heavenly tears and dew showers,
thirsted, scorched and weary,
while on yellow grassy paths
wicked evening eyes of sunlight
ran about you through dark trees,
blinding, glowing sunlight-glances, malicious?
...

FRIEDRICH NIETZCHE

Leftovers

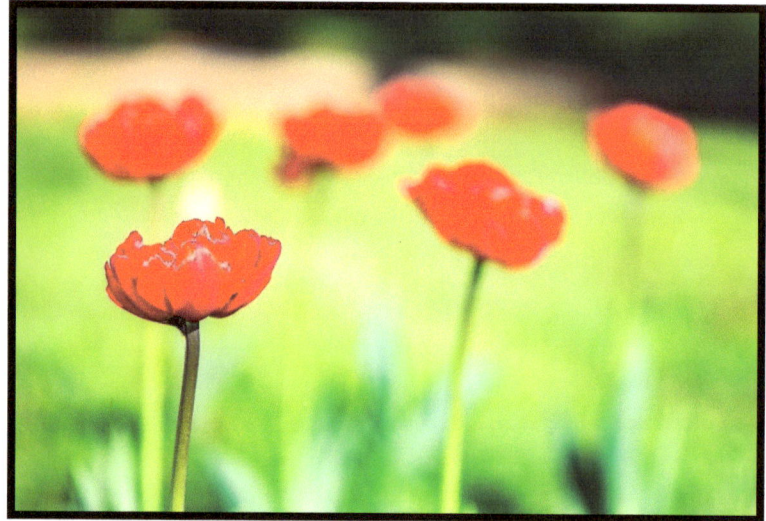

Red painted flowers

illuminated memoirs

summer leftovers

Hopeful

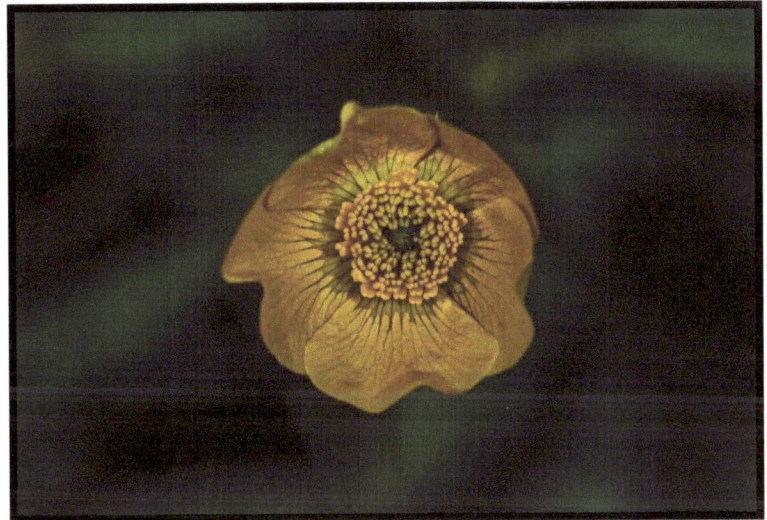

Bright yellow summons

the humming garden calms down

the grass smells hopeful

White dress

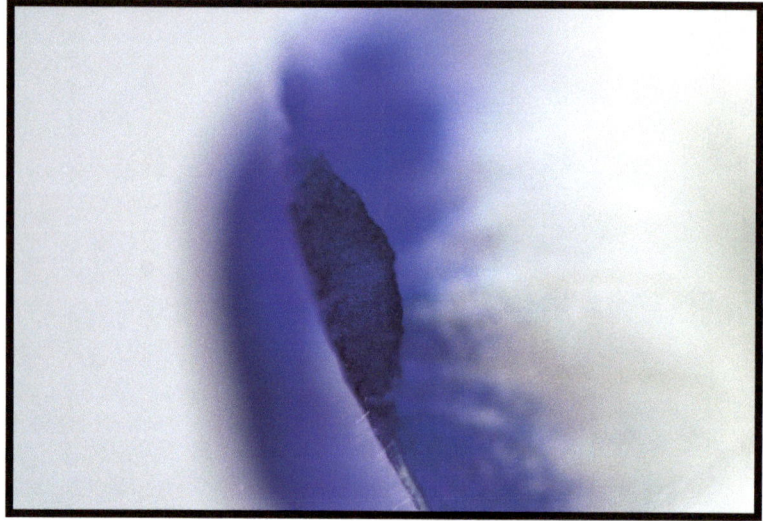

Delicate nature in a

midsummer's warm wave

elegant white dress

My mind

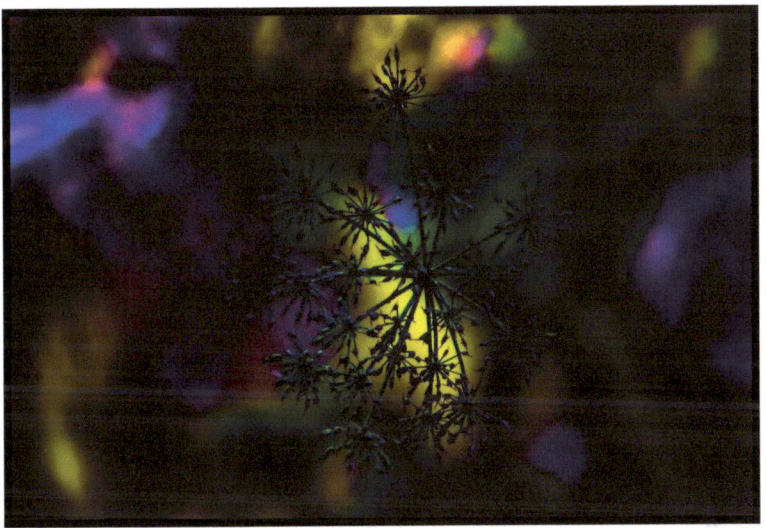

Wondering alone

starlight brightens the shadows

stirred in my mind

Transition

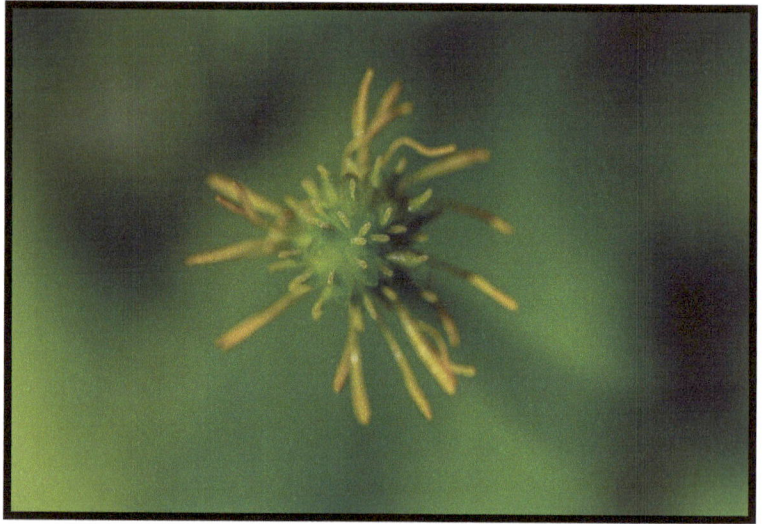

Between two natures

gaining closure losing now

a new transition

Unknown known

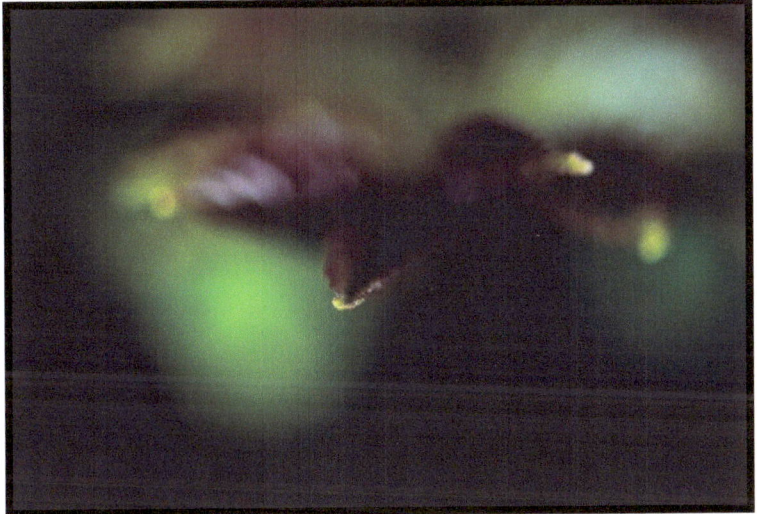

Retreating backwards

where the lights once were shining

to the unknown known

Bind

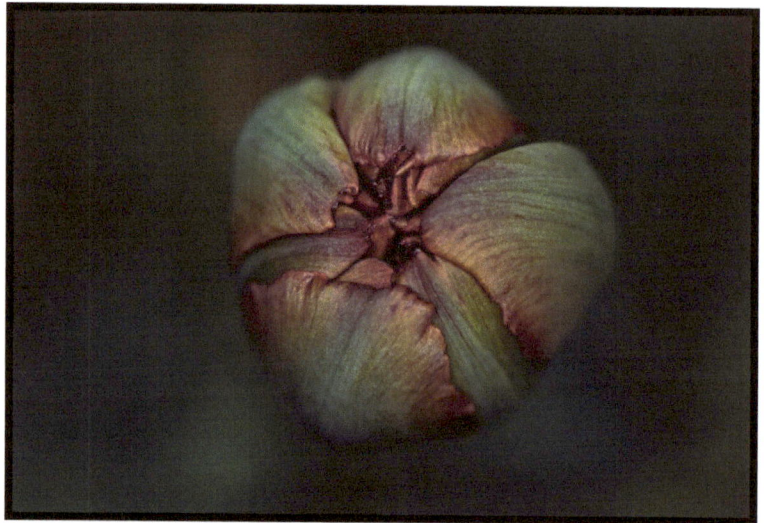

The dark ground silence

a changing time cries its spell

to cast off your bind

Paint it

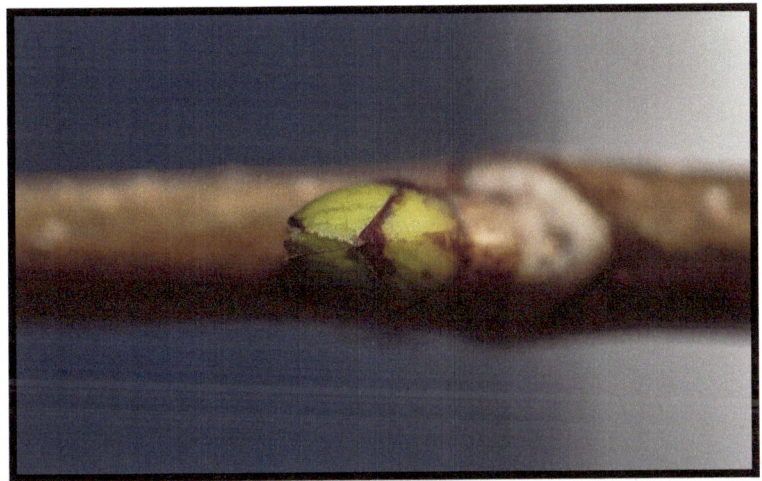

Being a brushstroke and shade's

deep colors, pressure, sudden turns

fading out

our hunger the blank canvas.

Certainly

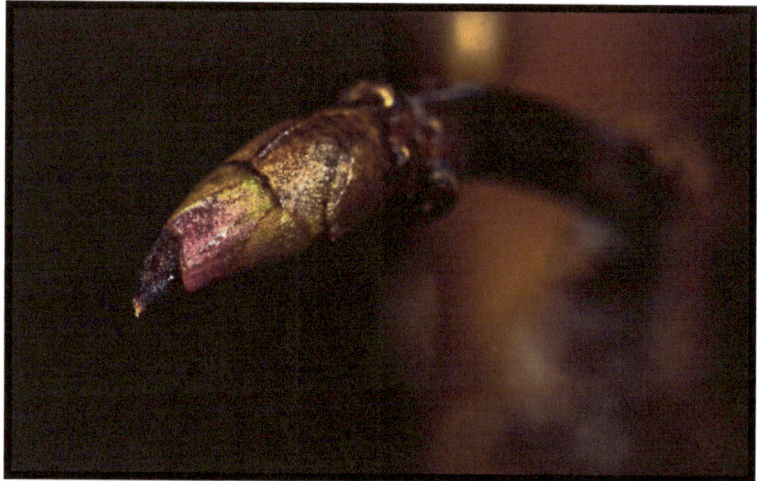

Nature colors like a painting

brush strokes lifted from a rich pallet

applied with a refined certainty

Autumn

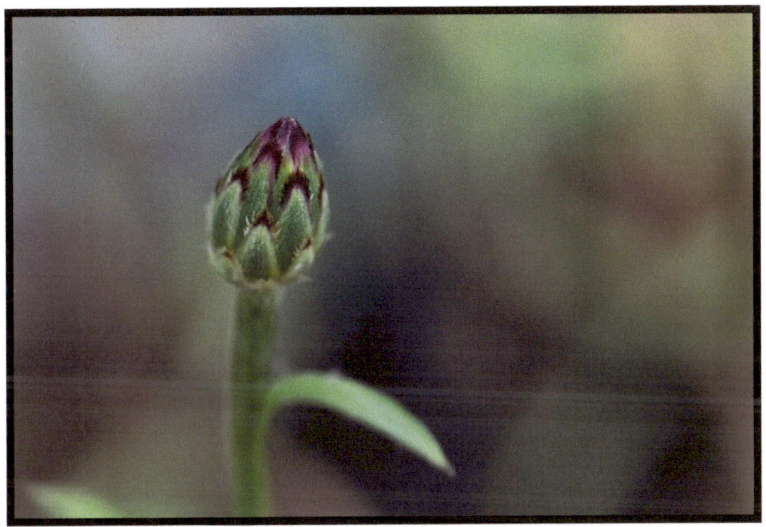

Delicate armor

layered to embrace a flower

to spring in autumn

Predicament

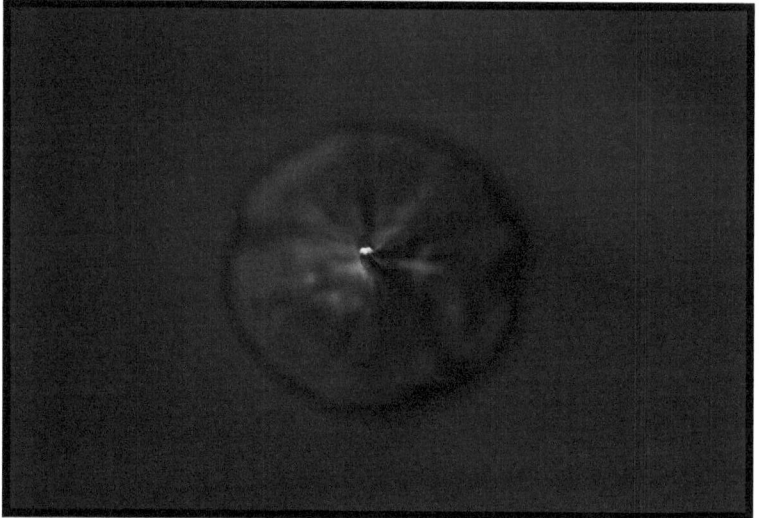

Awareness focused

vicinity fading out

a predicament

Nowhere to go

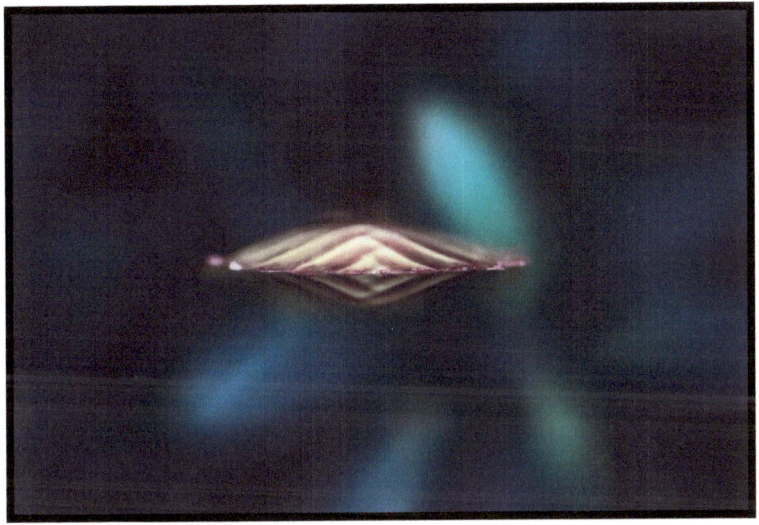

A lingering choice

then horizons multiply

and nowhere to go

Bends

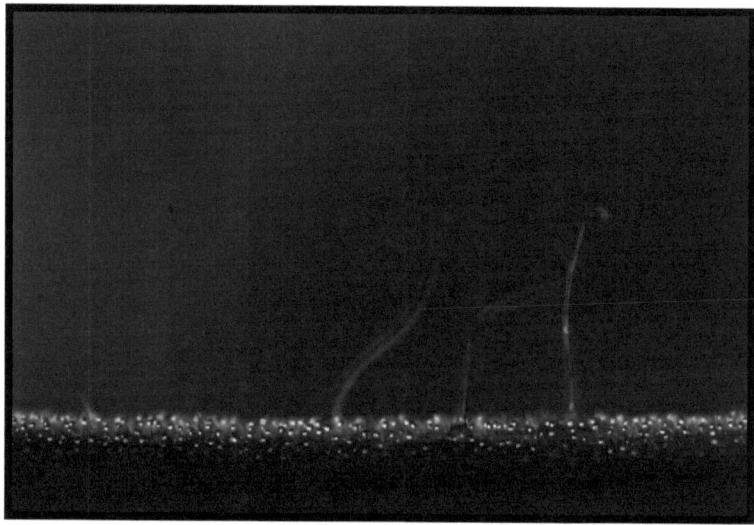

Too sensitive

if turbulent air directs

where the mind bends

A clue

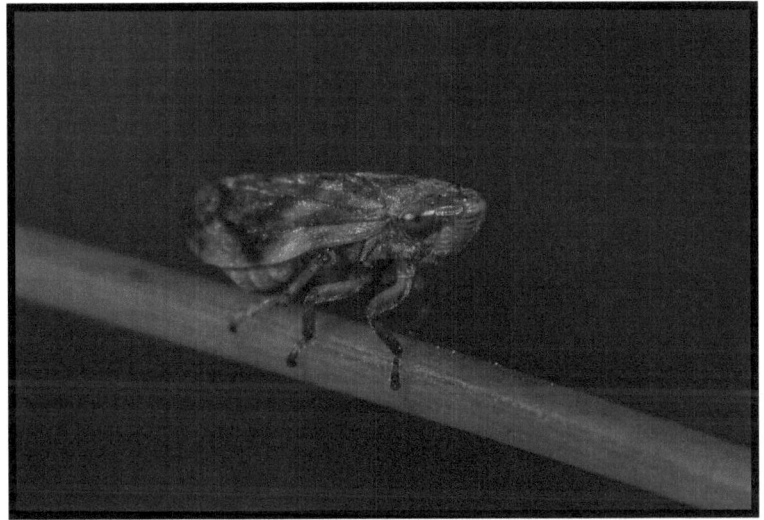

Holding on to tight

on a narrow path nowhere

protecting a clue

Pastures

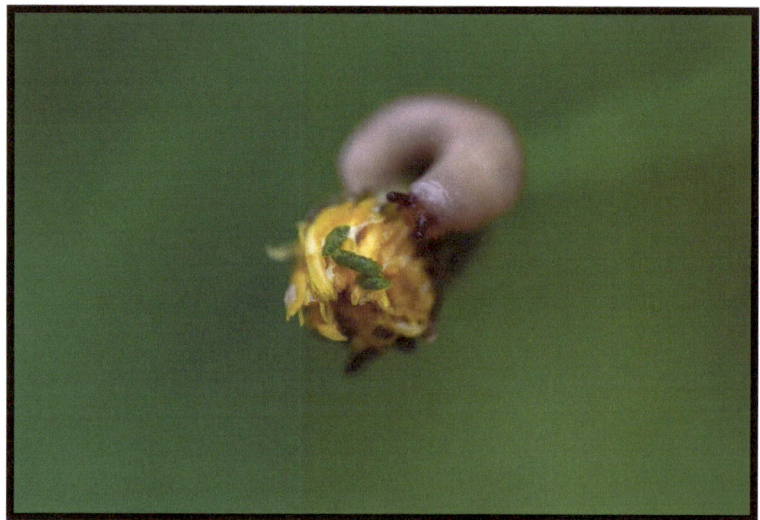

Slowly sliding up

for a meal at the ending

in lush green pastures

I return on

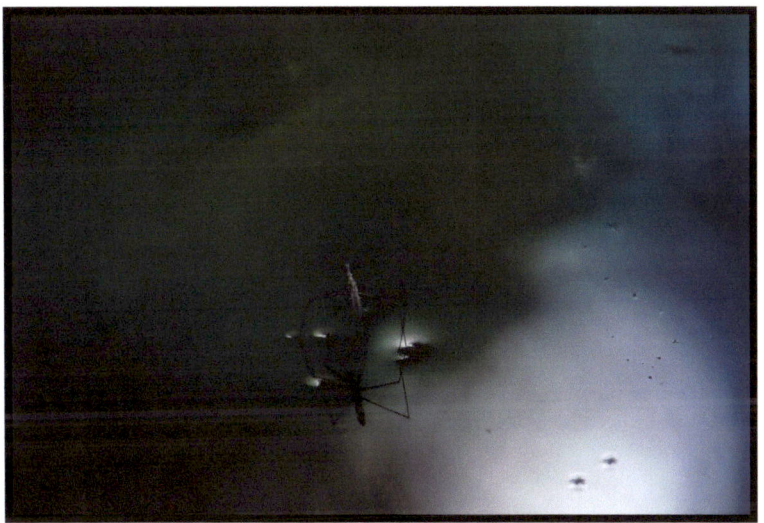

Colorful cover

reflecting onto my path

where I return on

Anticipating

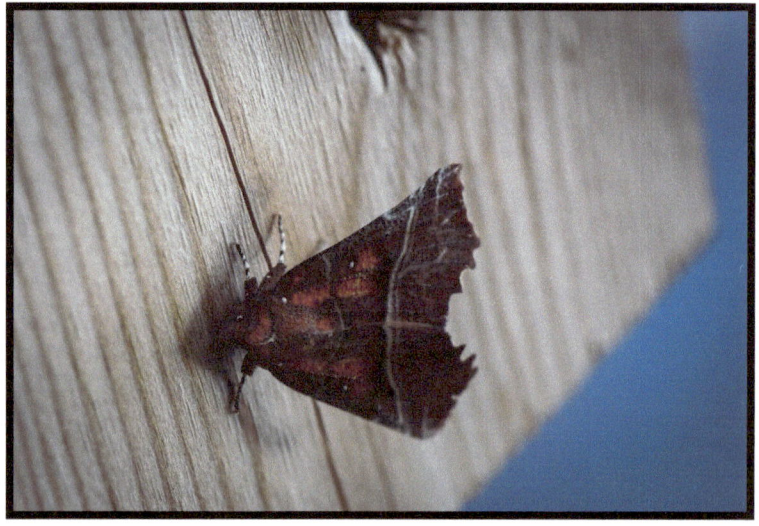

Wait on foreign soil

clinging on to the smallest

anticipating

Sun

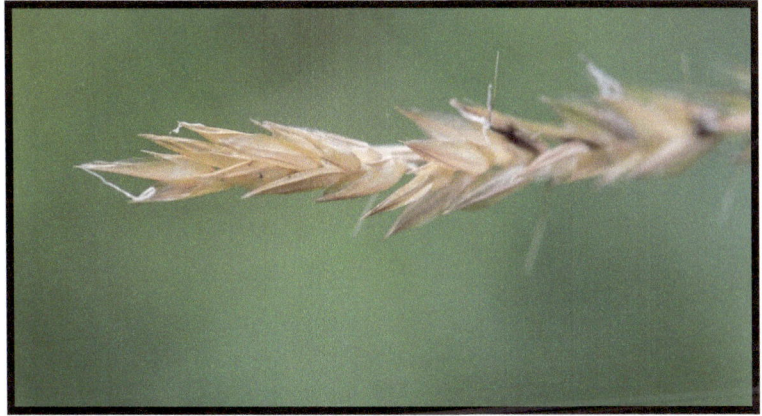

The wind is moving

bending wheat where it settles

in rough ground and sun

Riddles

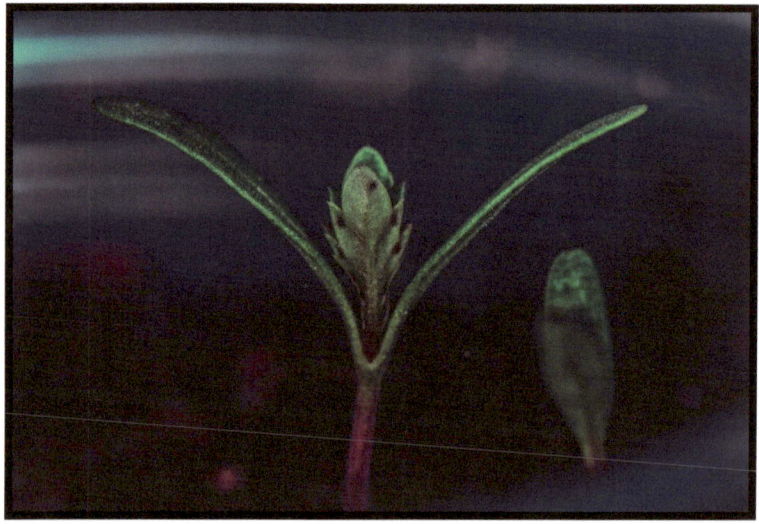

A youngling opens up,

to a world in riddles

Fragile

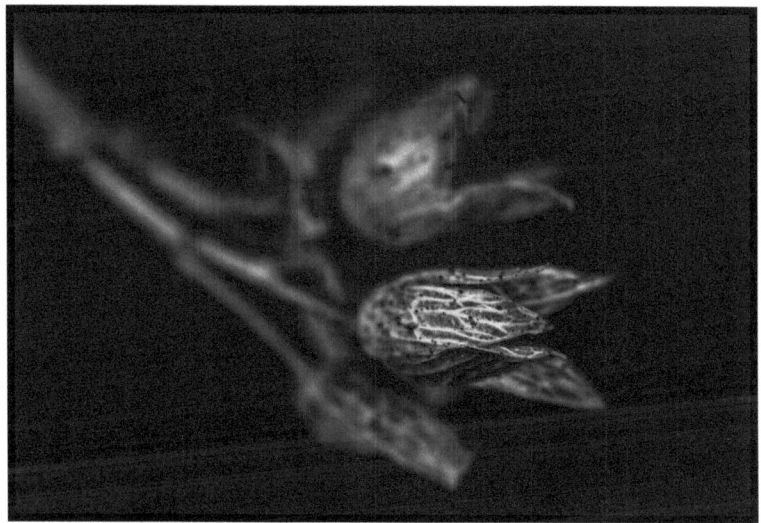

Porcelain nature still in time

Its ornate structure fulfilled willingly its purpose

fragile beauty before its decay

Longs

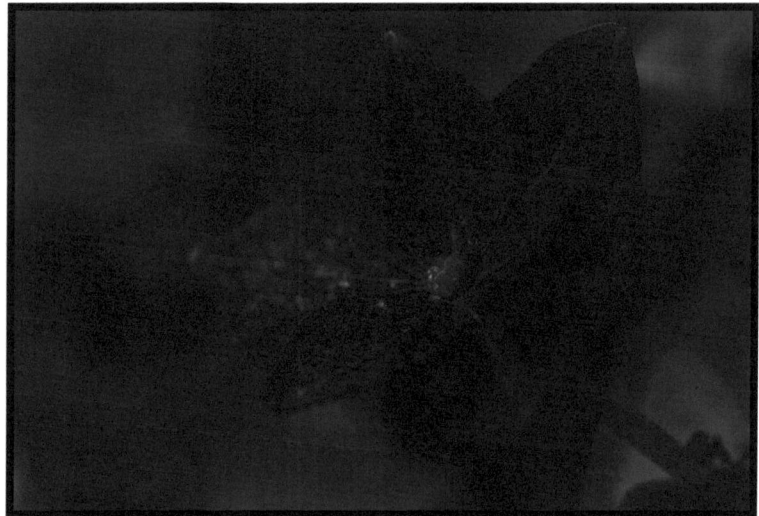

In darkened corners

growing in old fertile soil

a small flower longs

Feathers

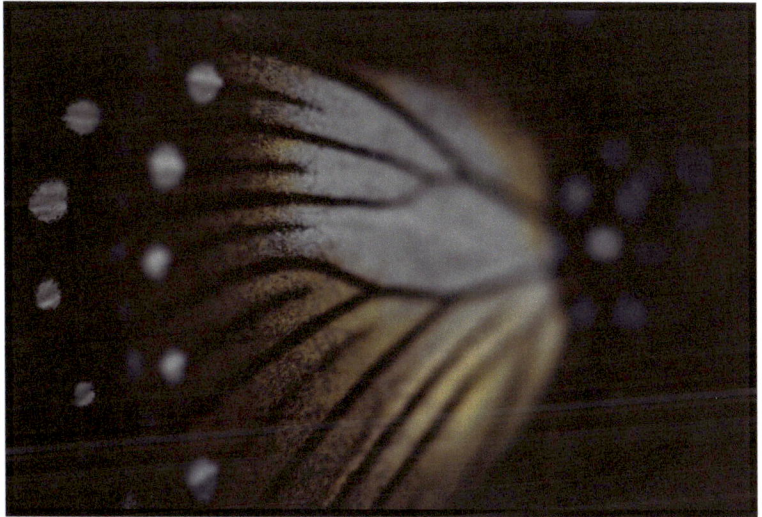

Unearthing a wing

forgotten somewhere beneath

collecting feathers

Cohesion ends

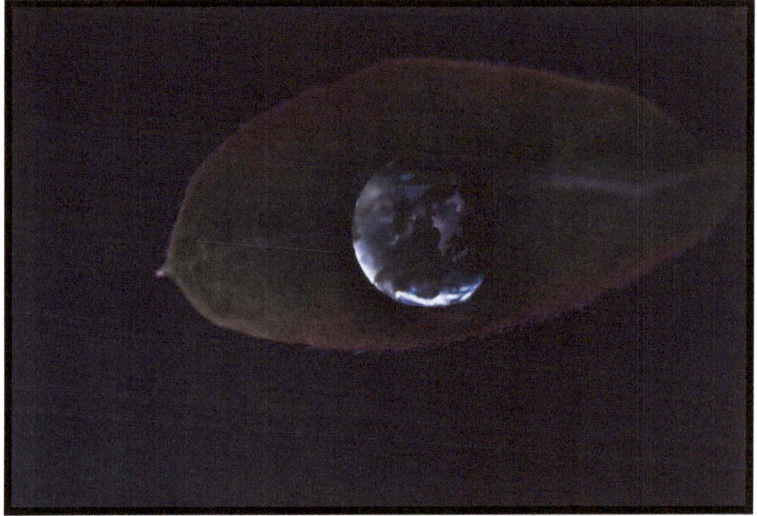

You reflect a world

still in equilibrium

till cohesion ends

Behind

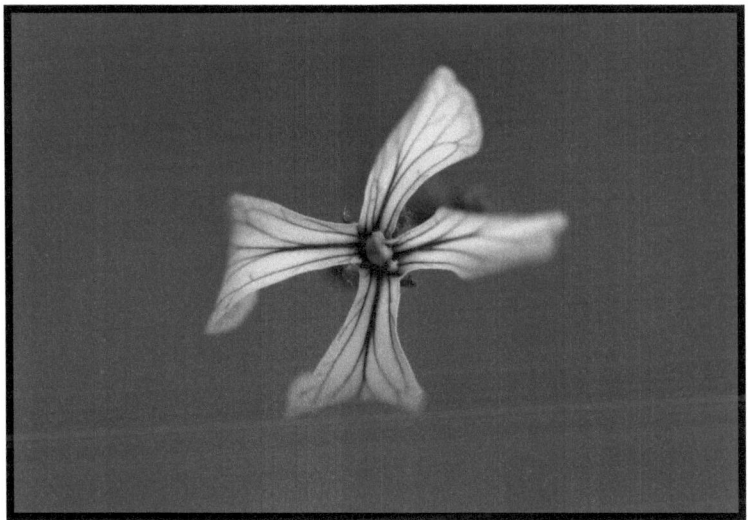

Grey sky surrounding

the wind drives you forwards

leaving you behind

Take over

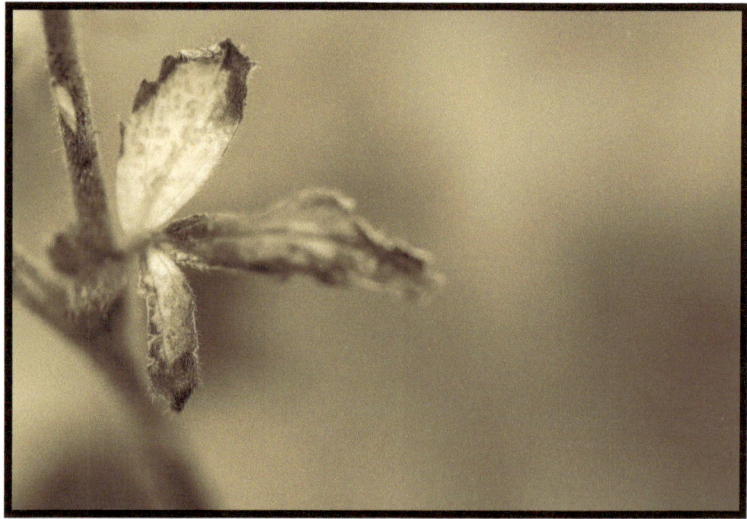

Morning light trough haze

the cold soil warms again

harsh lights take over

Storm

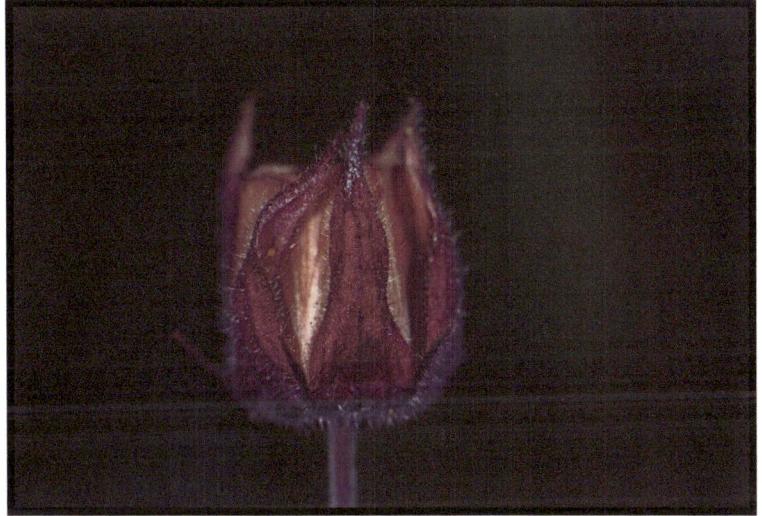

Fierce and proud standing

with a frail and graceful stance

to weather the storm

To the rim

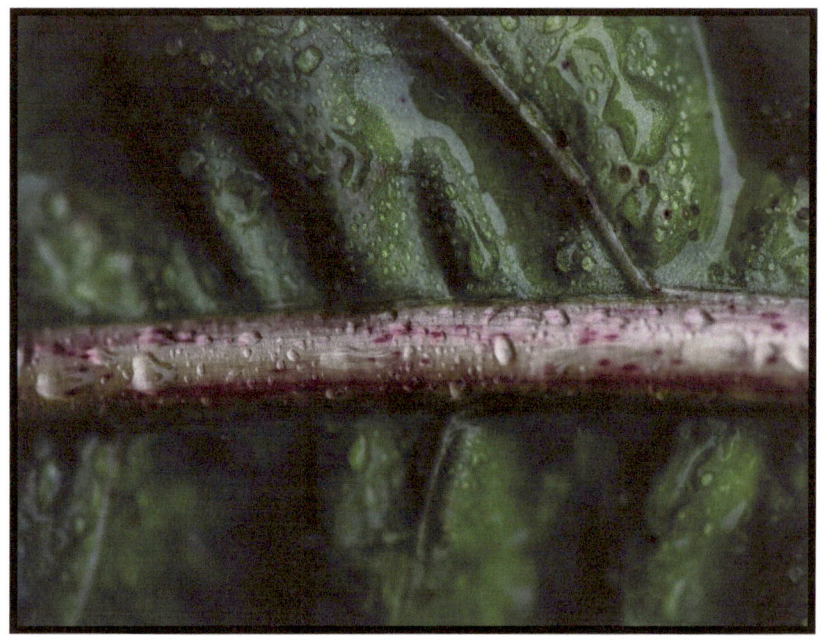

Rivers emanate

from a shoot within my mind

downhill to the rim

Shatters

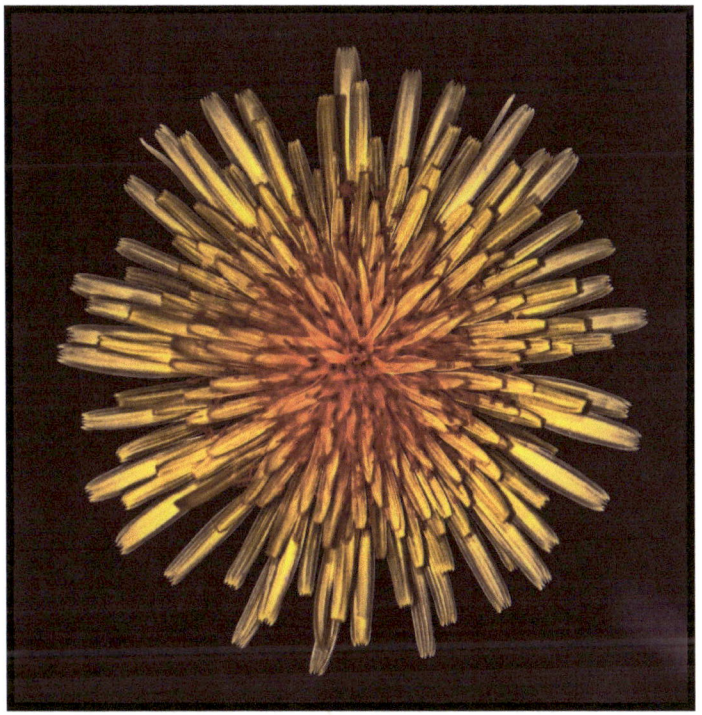

The instant movement

when shades fade in the distance

and your star shatters

Scent of summer

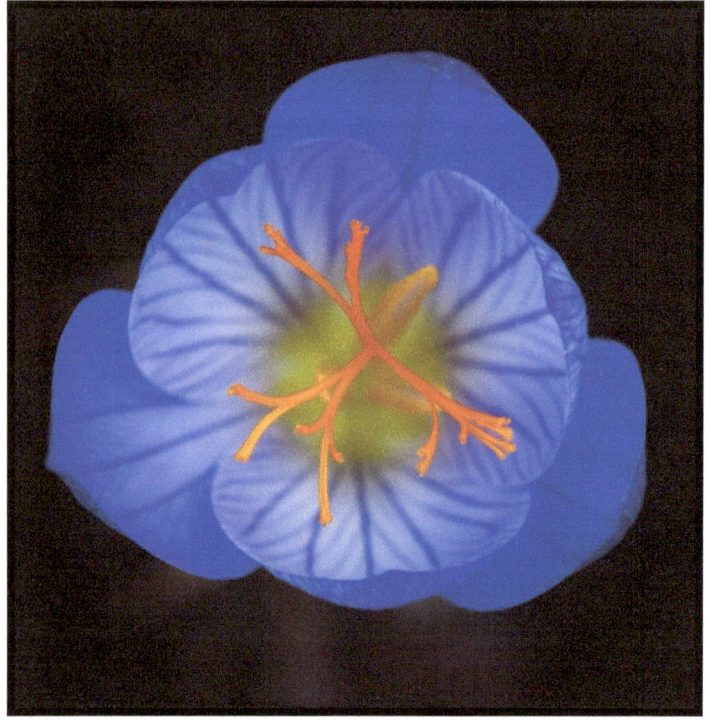

A light blue cocoon

slowly opens when it reveals

a scent of summer

Cracks

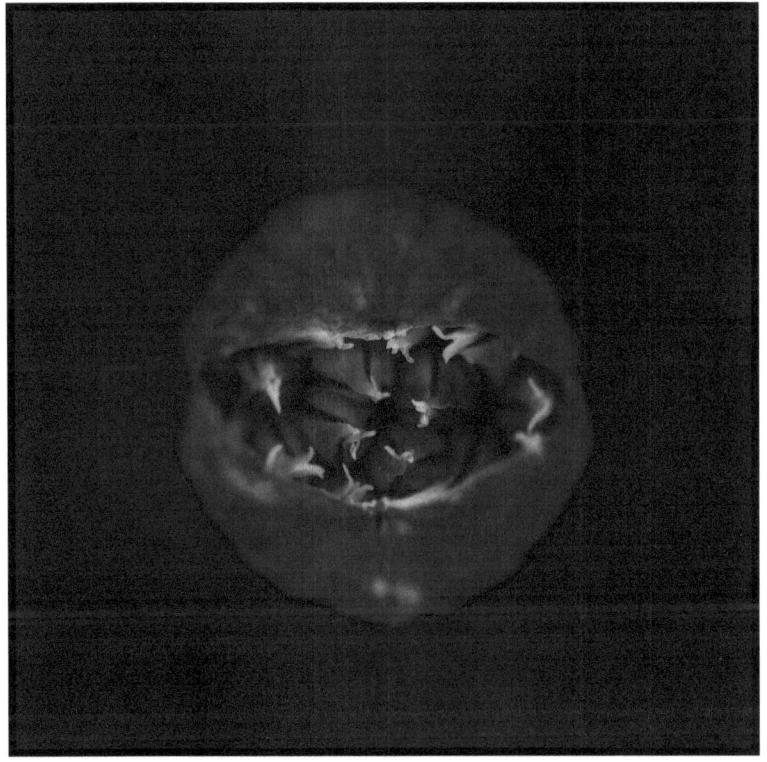

The louvres open

and I peer out the window

through inviting cracks

Black hole

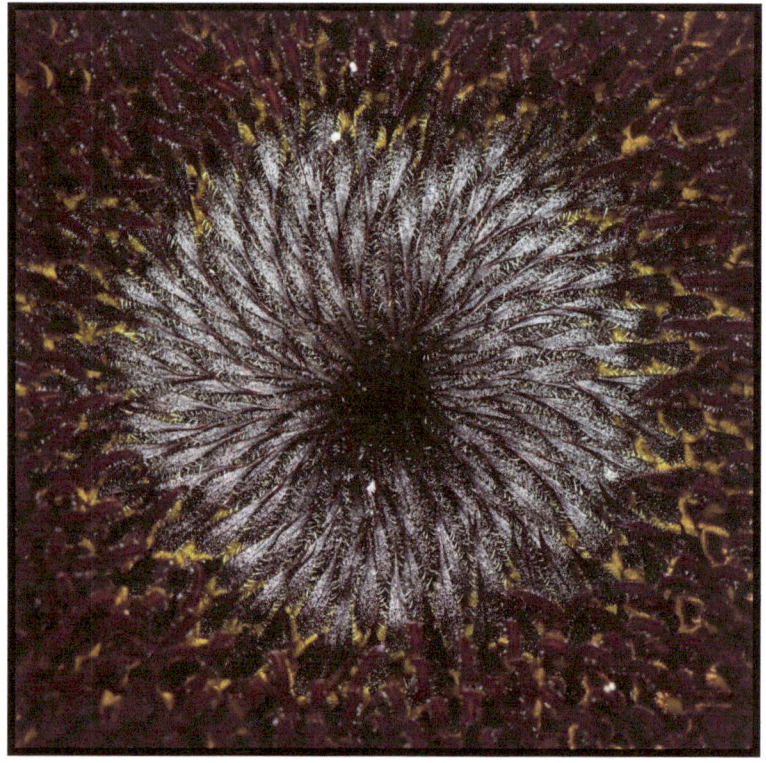

Reality fades

caught by egos gravity

a depressed black hole

Tangled

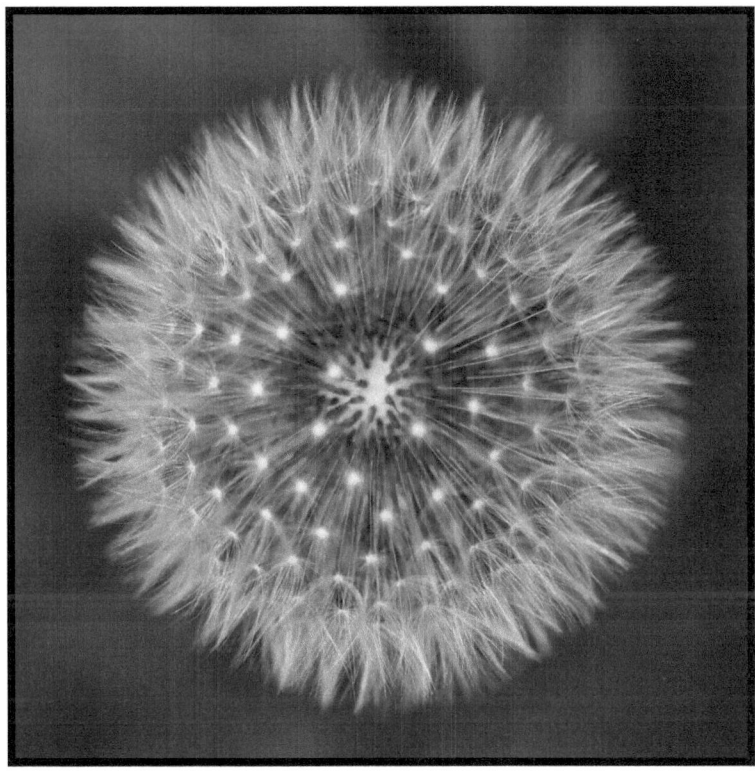

Towards the outside of my awareness

the transition is veiled

reality and imagery are tangled

Sleep

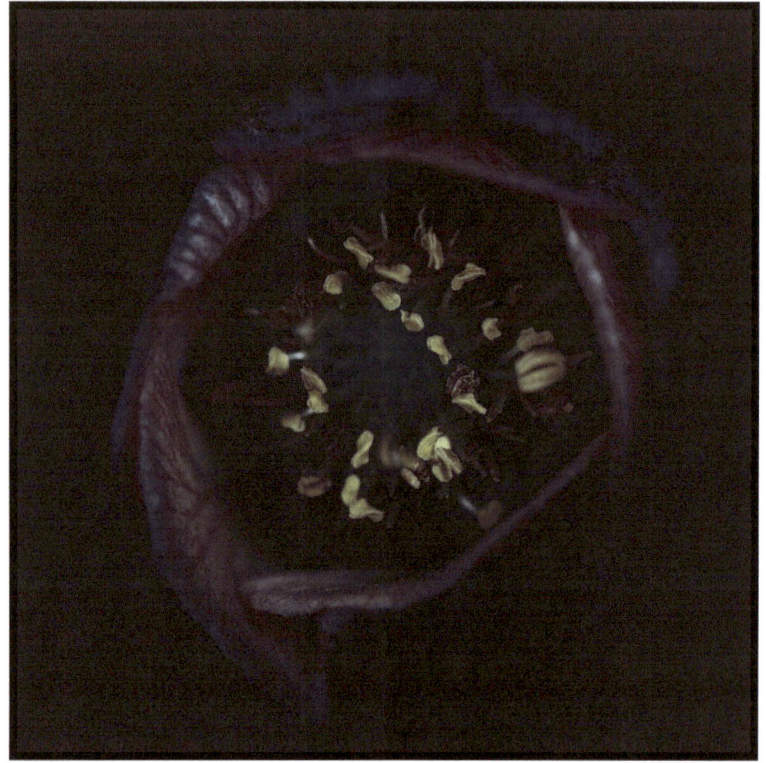

A shell to preserve

when the light is retreating

and the bees do sleep

Façade

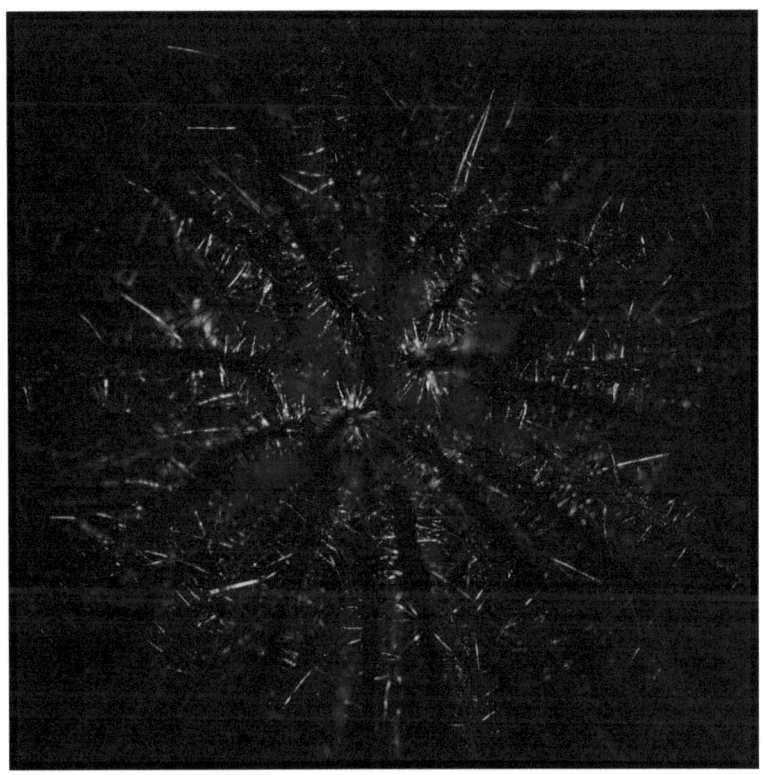

Turn slowly inside

let go what's within to me

your unknown façade

Giving it back

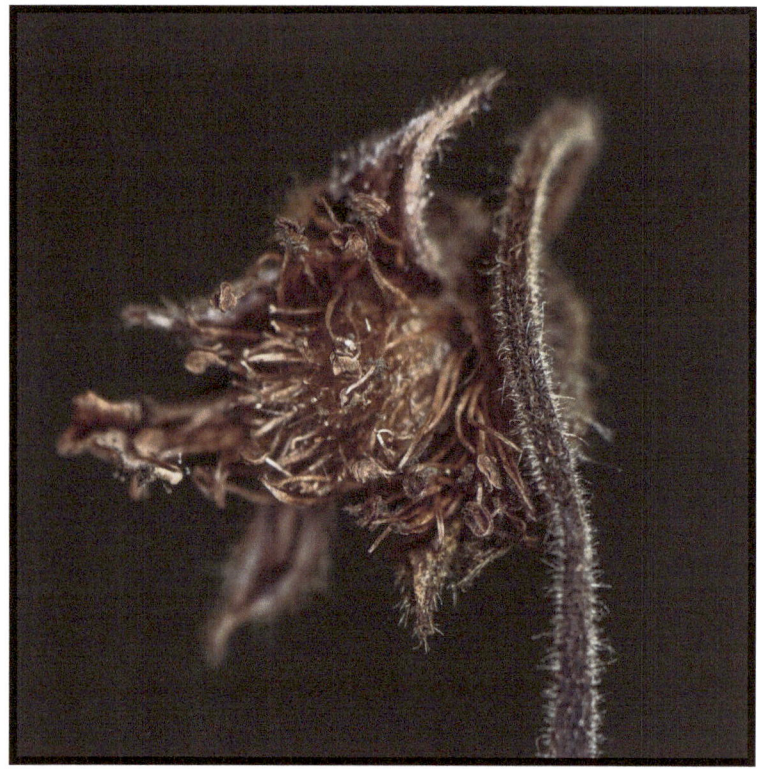

Waiting for the ground

absorbing time, decisions

and giving it back

In

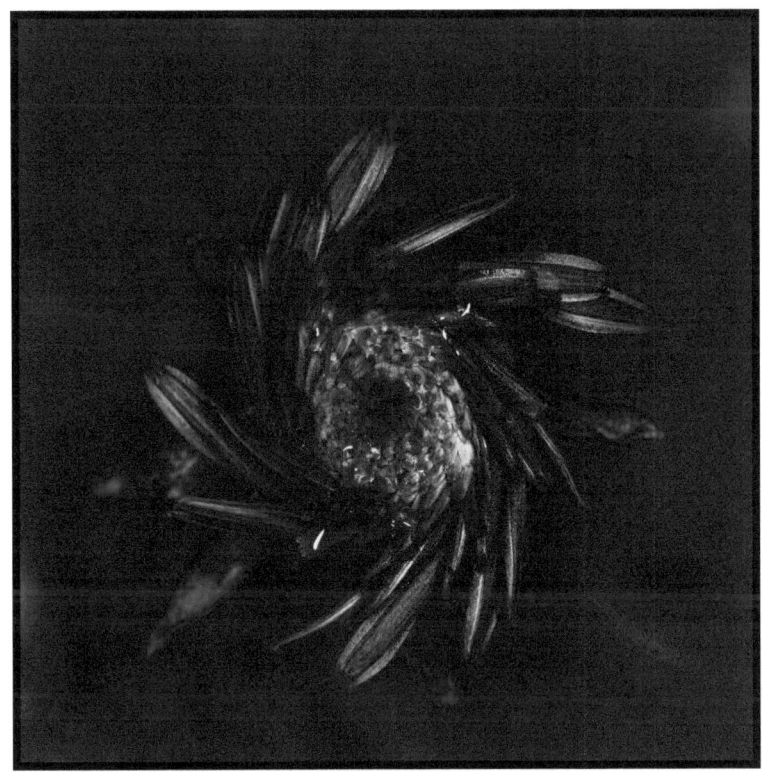

Eyes closed and the darkness spirals

the black mass pulls down, up, it turns,

the movement lures my mood in

Rhythm

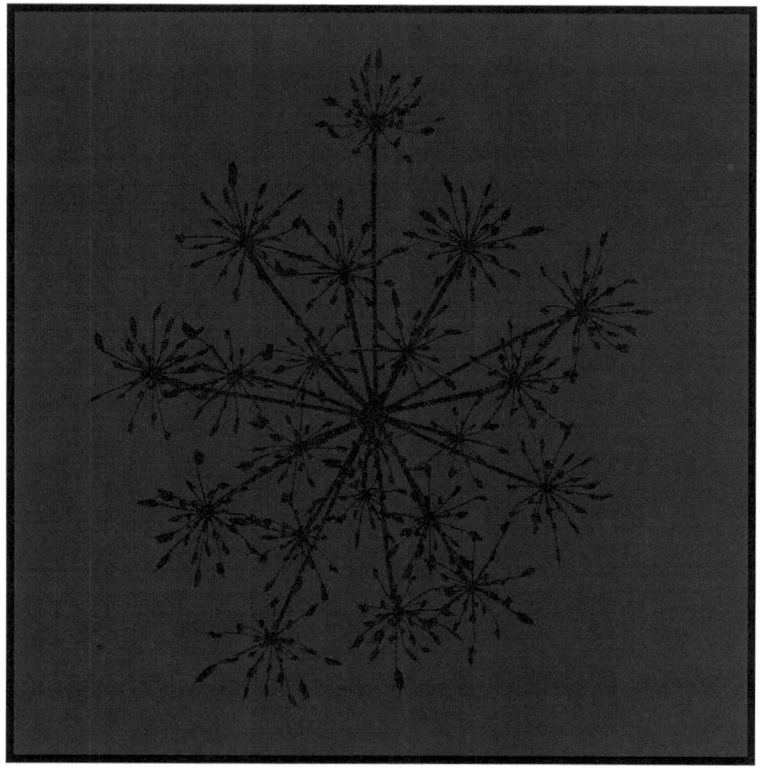

I spread my fingers

trying to touch entirety

its hidden rhythm

Farewell

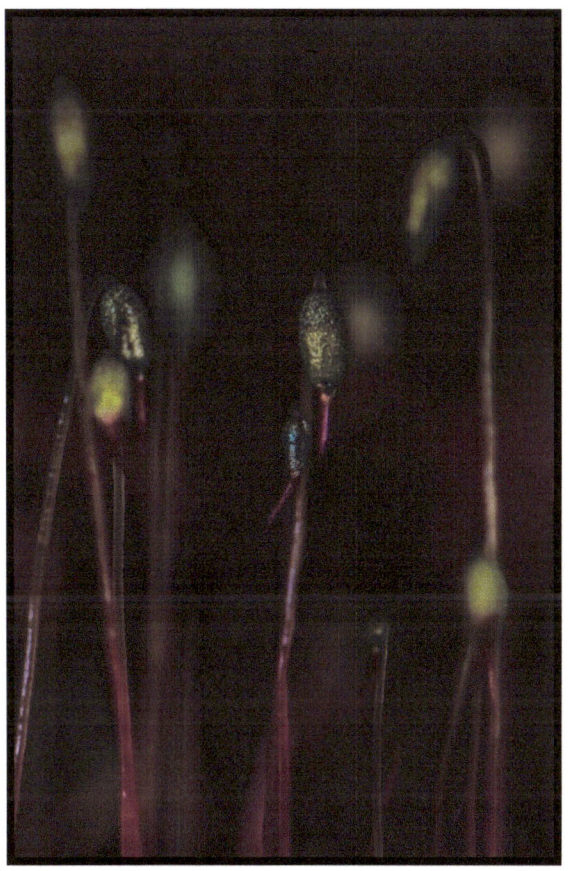

Standing together consoling with grief

last summer's joy grey lifeless before us

a final dark moment farewell

Liftoff

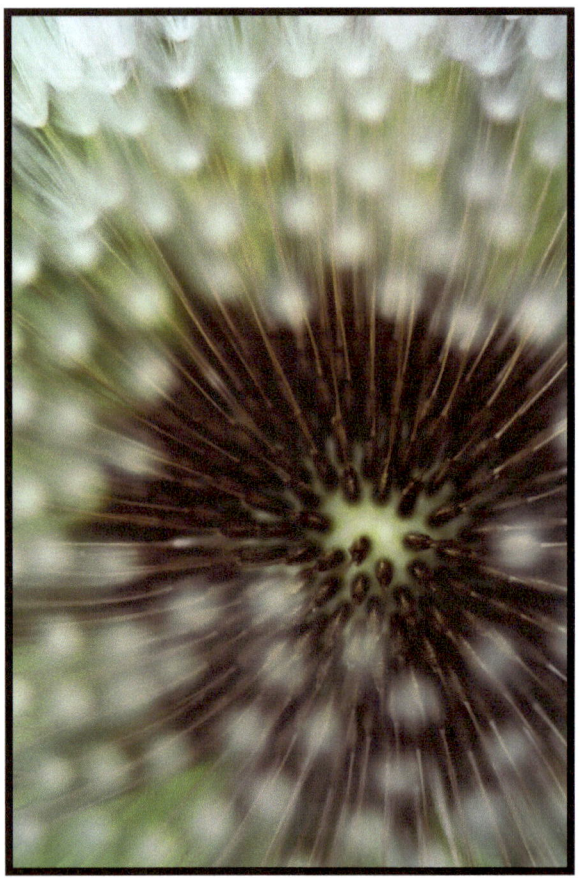

Bustling factory

impregnated multitudes

wanting to liftoff

Flow

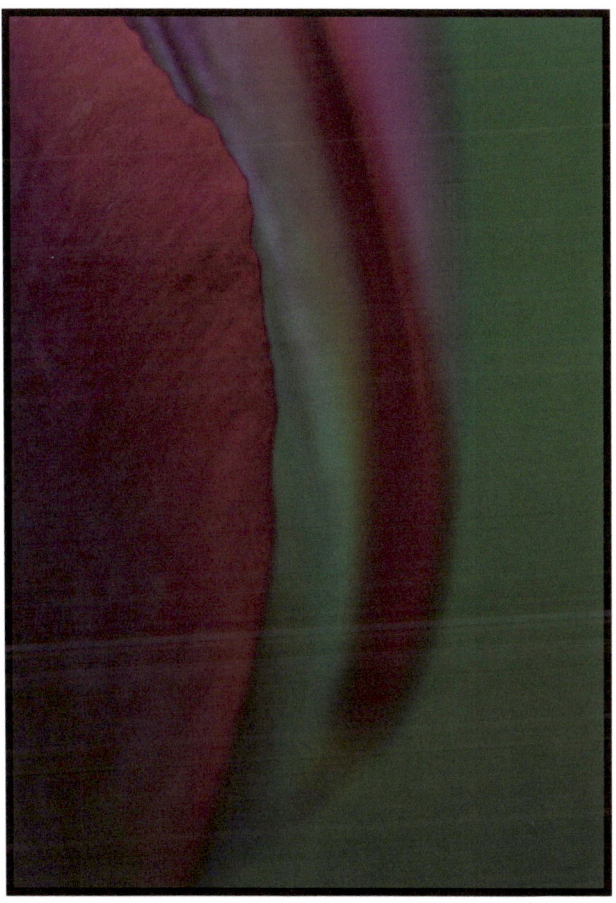

Red lines green nature

sharp strokes divided colors

inner natures flow

The sun

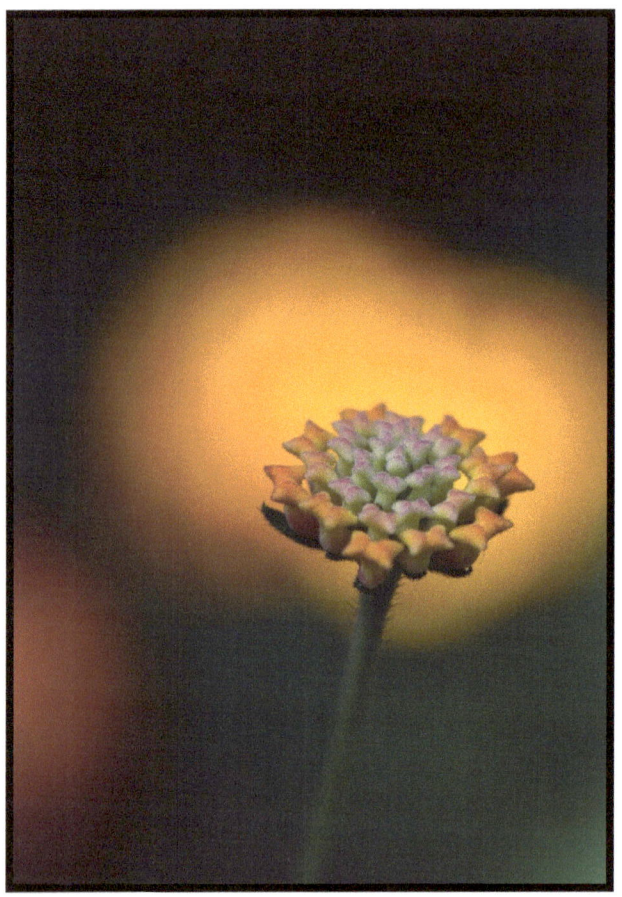

A colorful crown

imagined by time gone by

sprouted with the sun

Slowing down

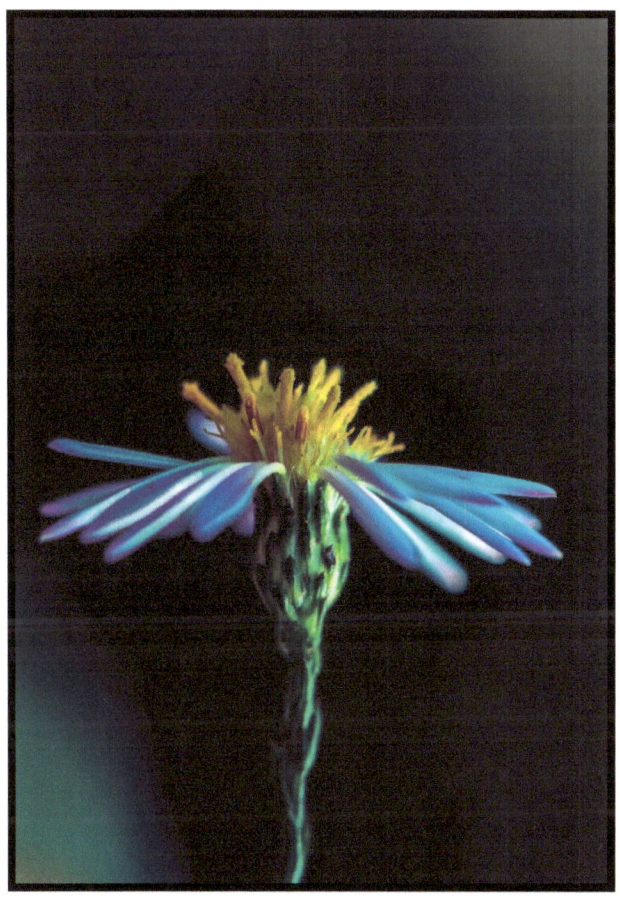

I spiral and turn

trusted upwards feeling free

a past slowing down

Leave me here

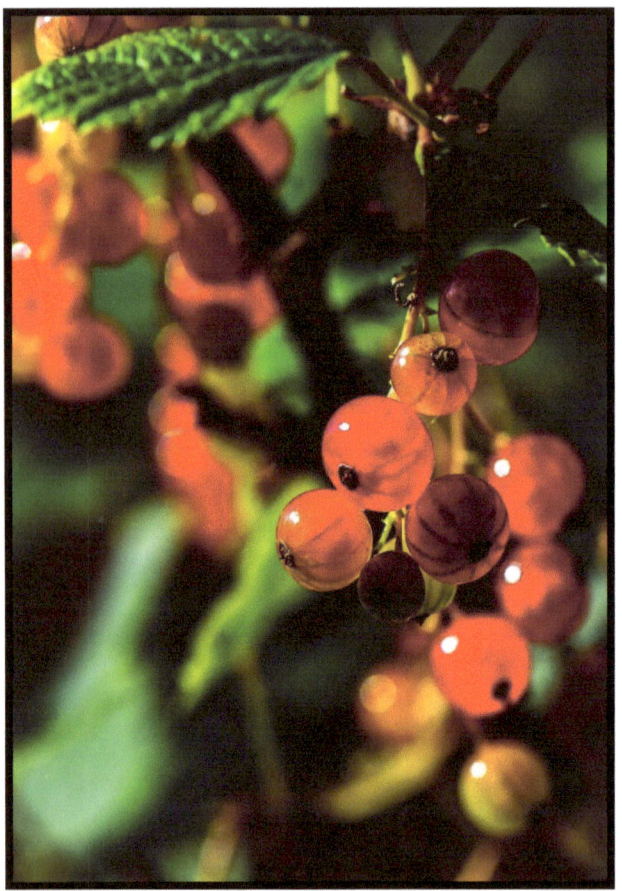

Red berries in the sun the air

smells from afternoon rain let

me forget and stand still and

leave me here

Grass

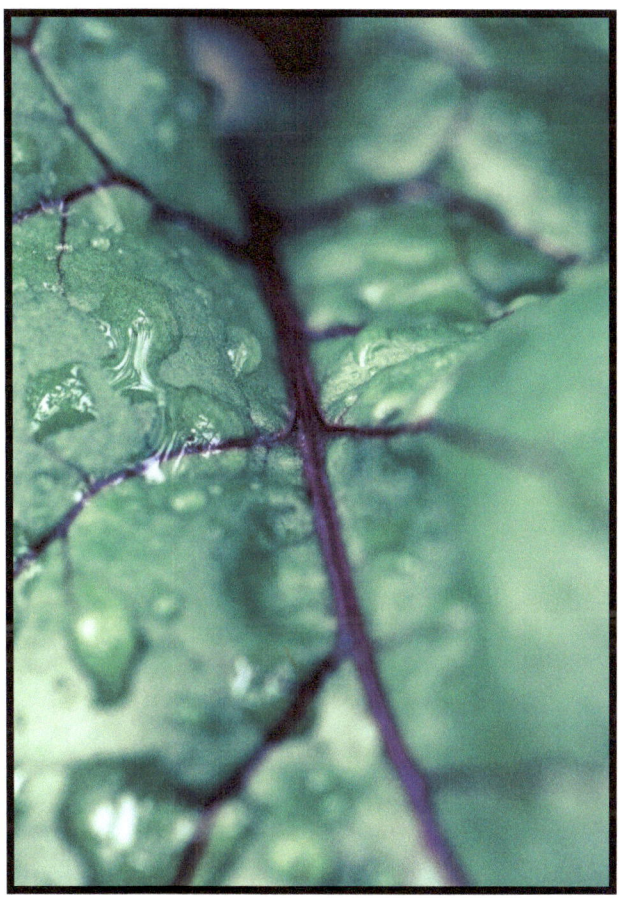

Waterfalls silent

scene from a distend valley

a hand in moist grass

Spread out

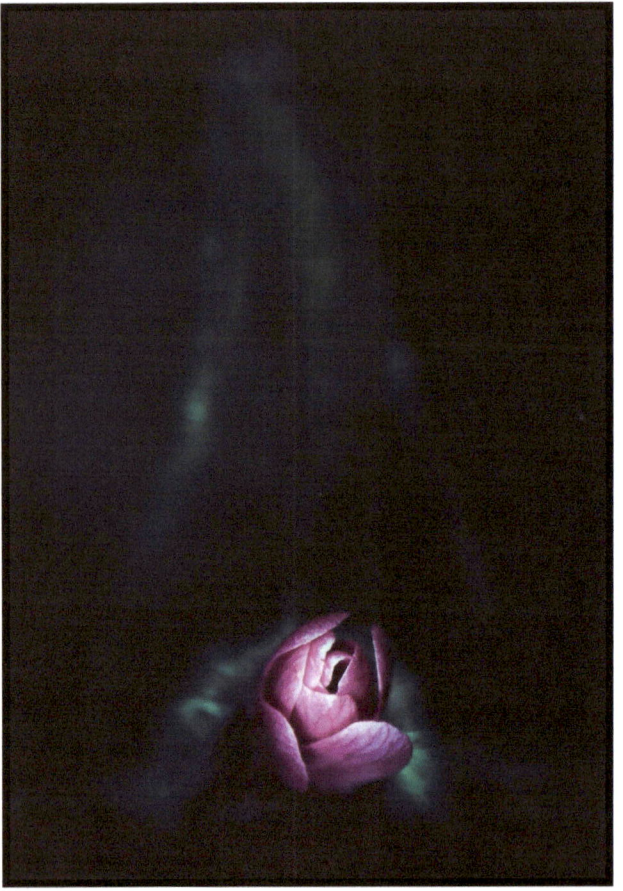

A newborn rises

from green darkened surroundings

to charm and spread out

To the end

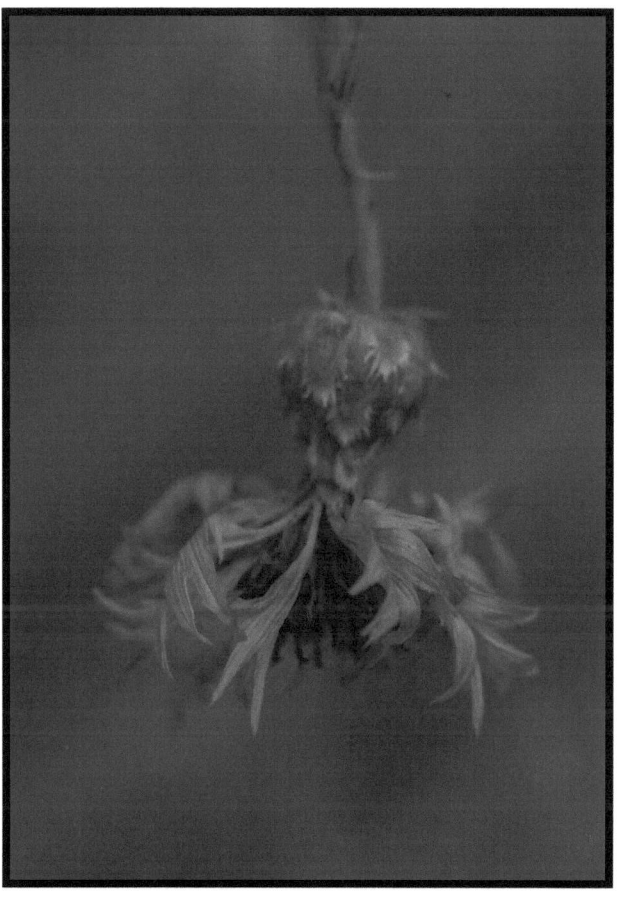

Beauty slowing down

gentle, a flower withers

swirling to the end

Virgin colors

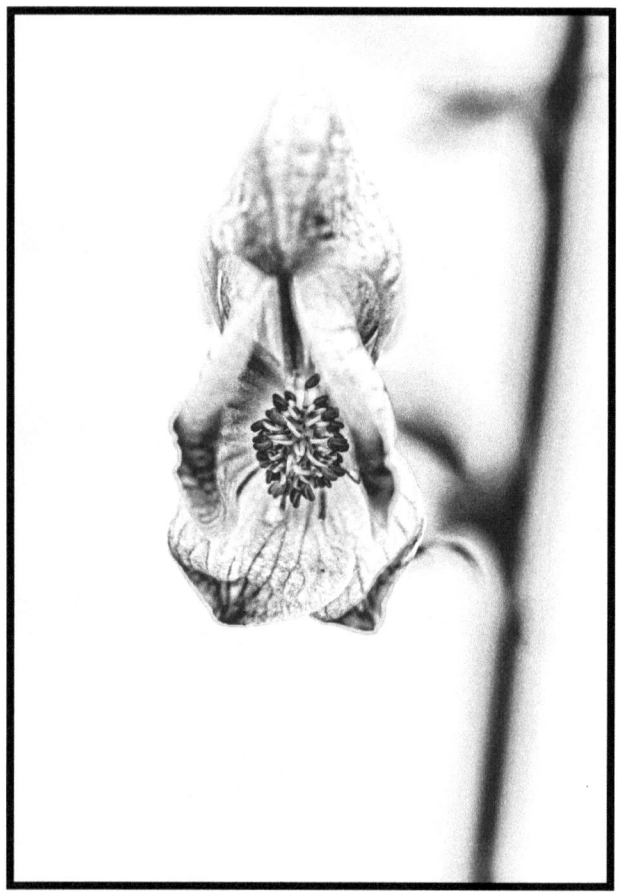

Alluring symbols

assessed by many facets

in virgin colors

Receding

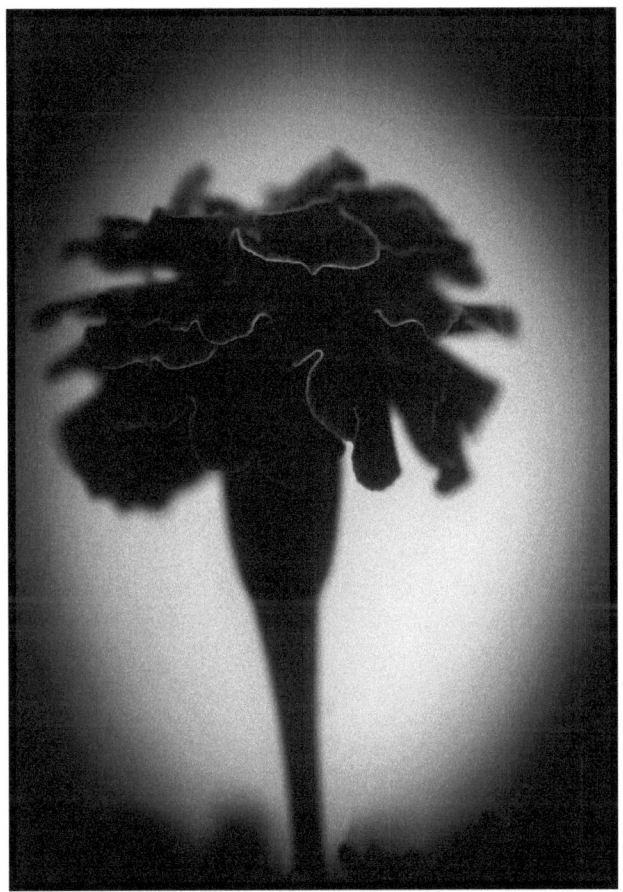

Light shines a corner

a dreaming line fades this dawn

black veils receding

I look up

Wall of thoughts in front

echoing sentences fall

frightened I look up

Moments

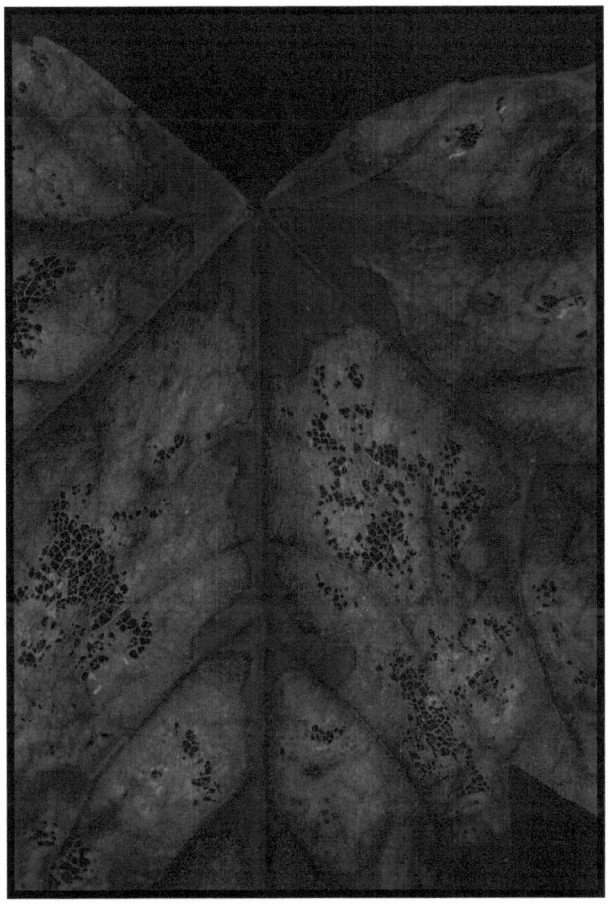

Receding into

memories of green seasons

decomposed moments

Stale air

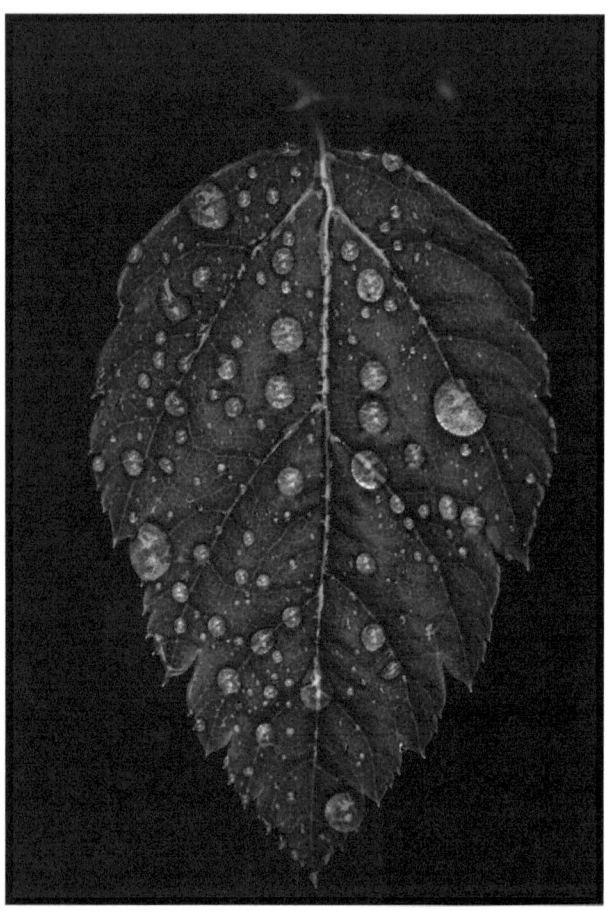

Adhesion for now

after falling from afar

in bitter stale air

Out

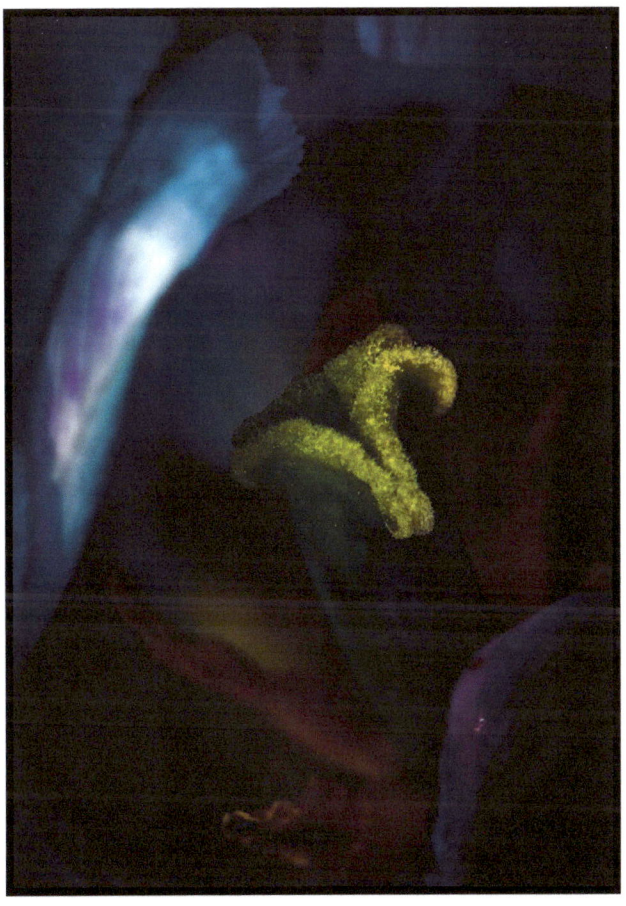

From darkness recess

wild colors surge and explode

to drown it all out

The mirror

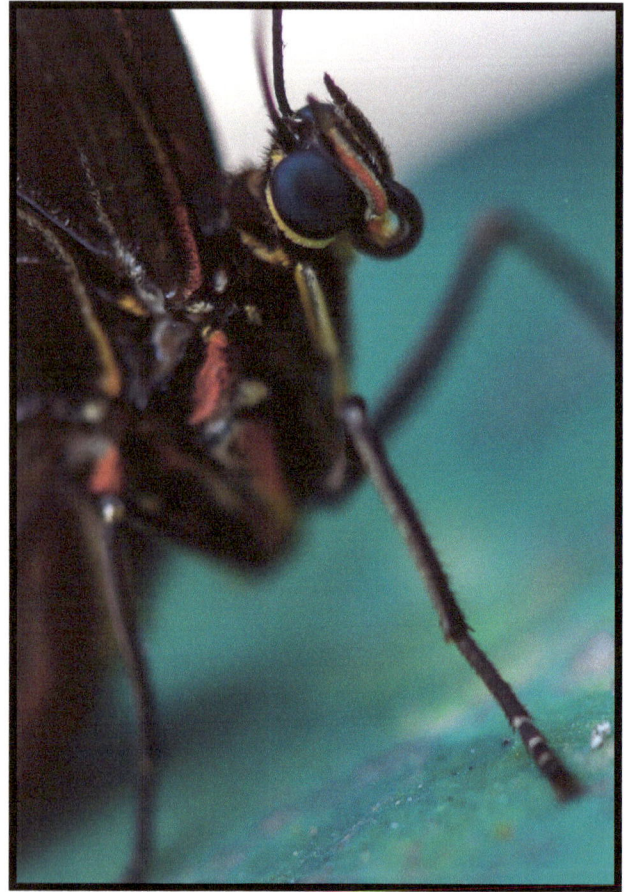

I see a stranger

my hairs rise and with my fear

I turn the mirror

Colors

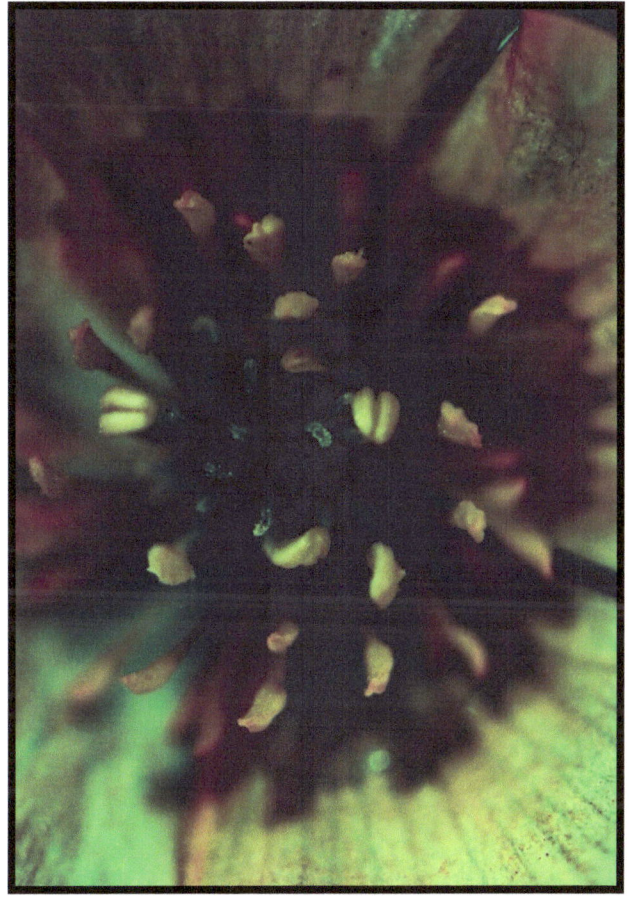

A colorful eye

closing for incoming light

for richer colors

Disperse

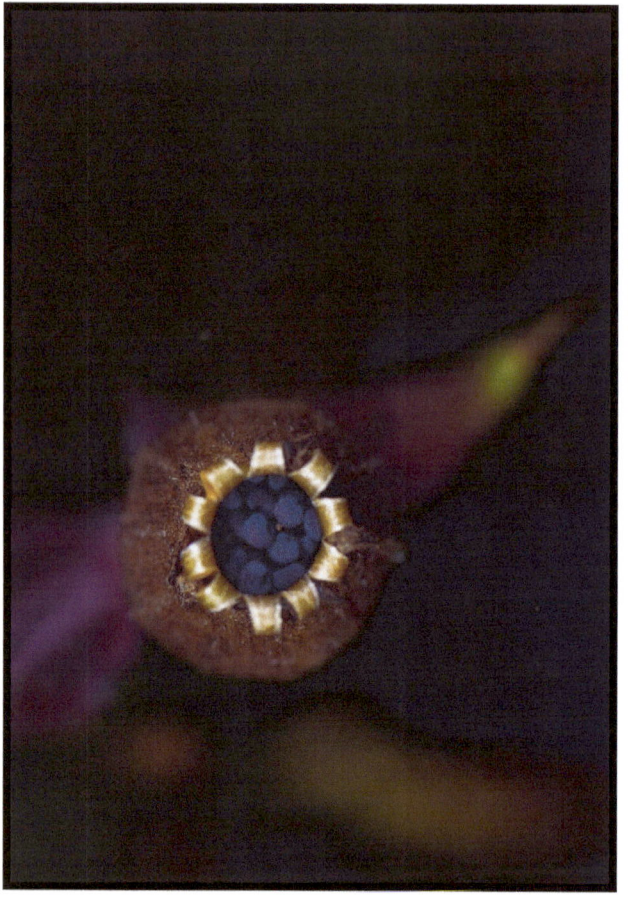

Upwards to gather

light that pulls up to the blue

where seeds can disperse

The wind

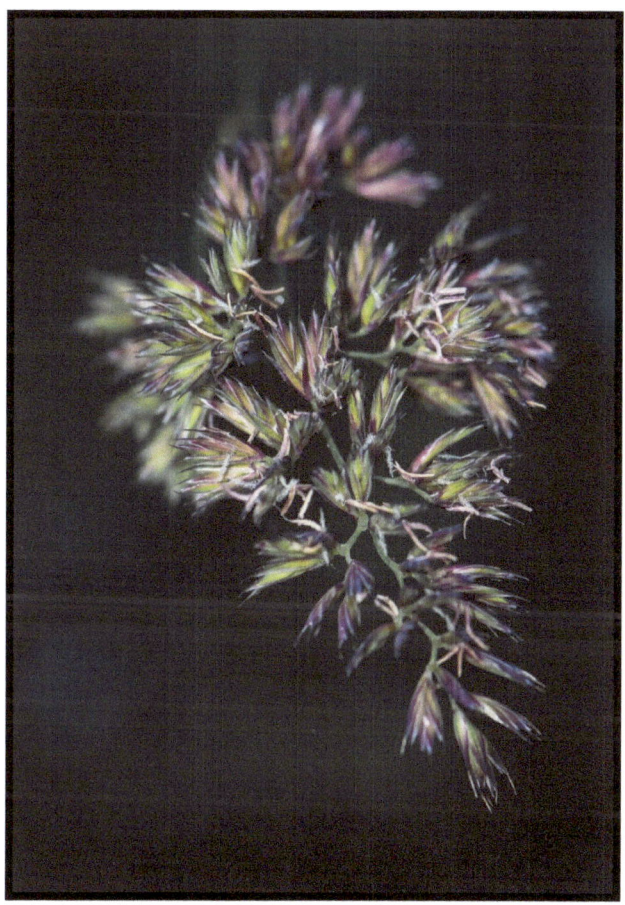

My nature goes out

and in focus at random

changing with the wind

Passing's

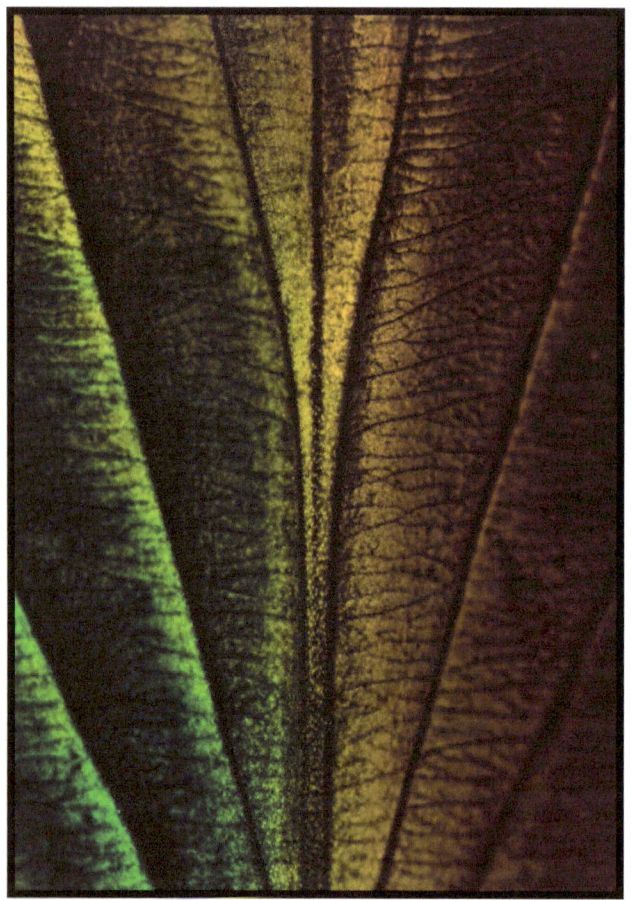

Shifting leaf colors

in these morning autumn drives

beautiful passing's

New path

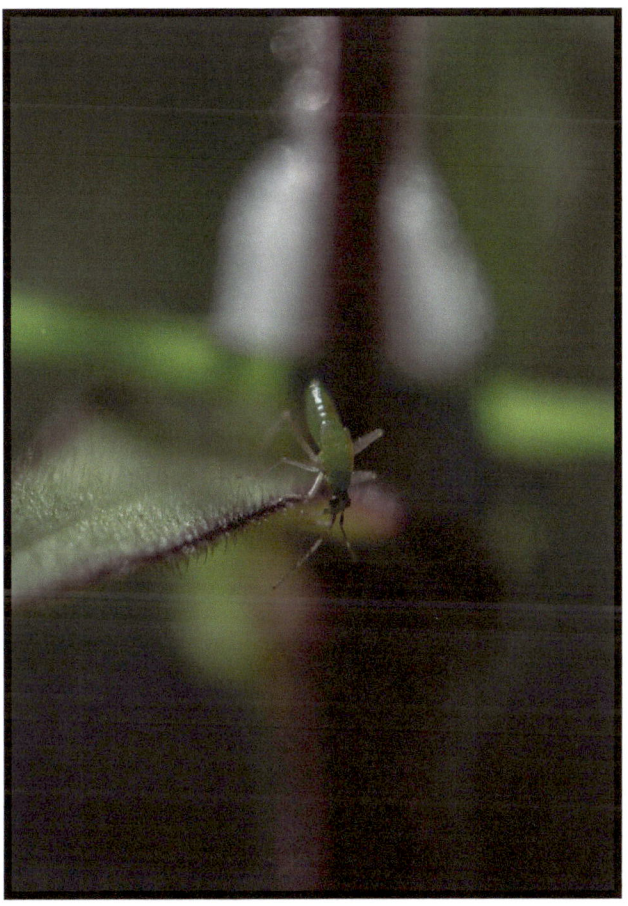

A Little mind thinks

what mystery have we here

under this new path

Wide open

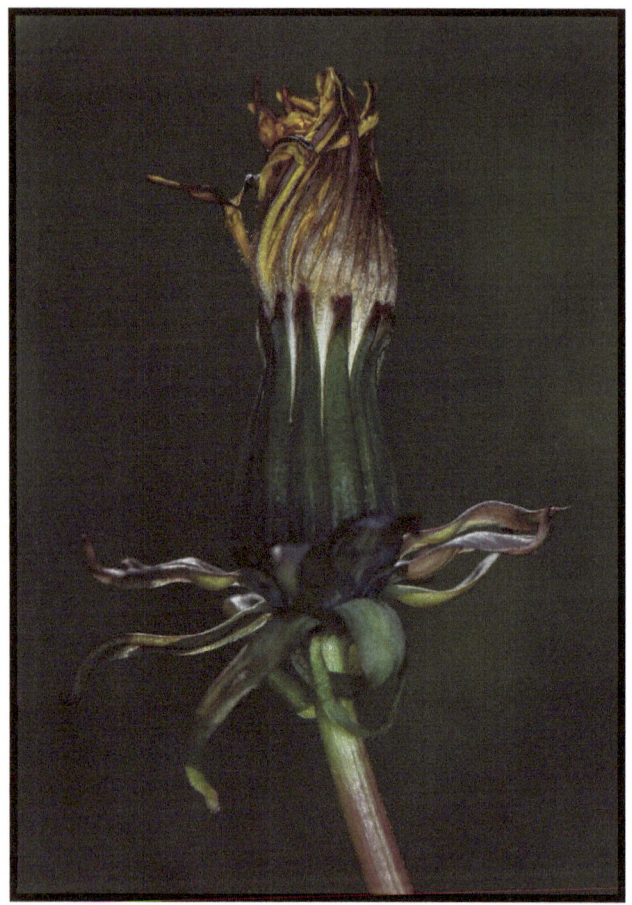

Charmingly dirty

enthusiastically

eyes still wide open

Never bloom

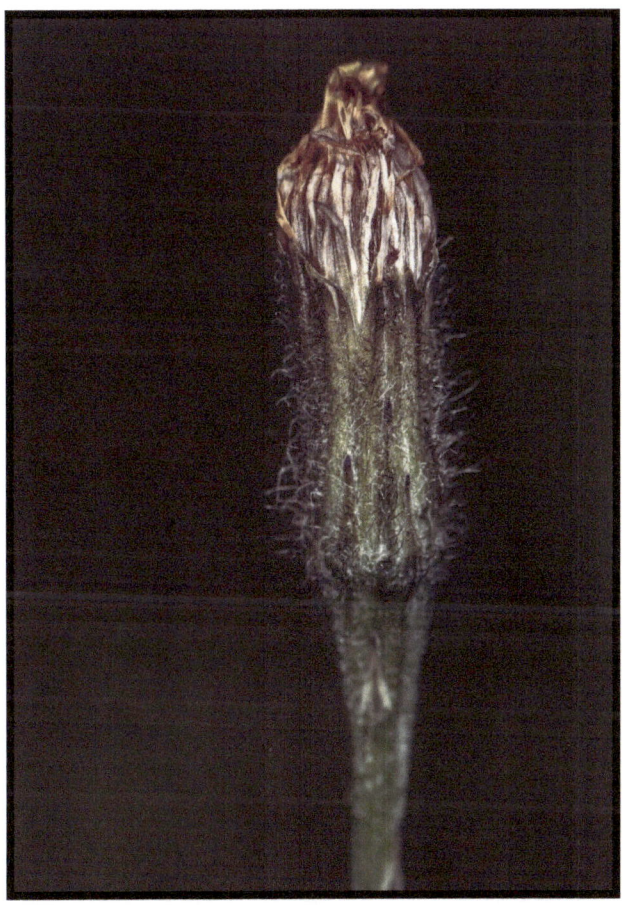

The sun is too late

shrouded in drawn out shadows

it will never bloom

Looms

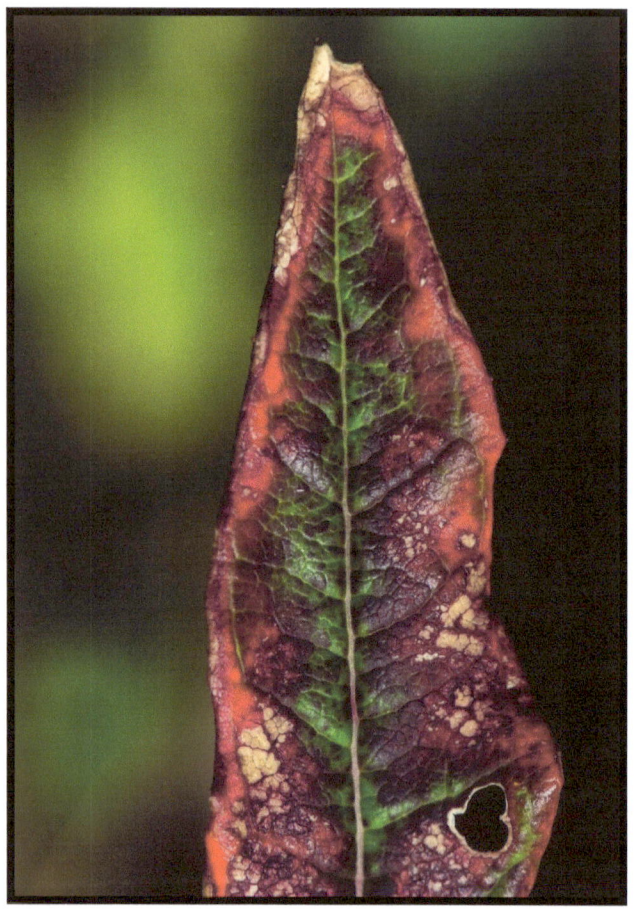

Habitual fall

when festering thoughts rain down

transformation looms

Shade

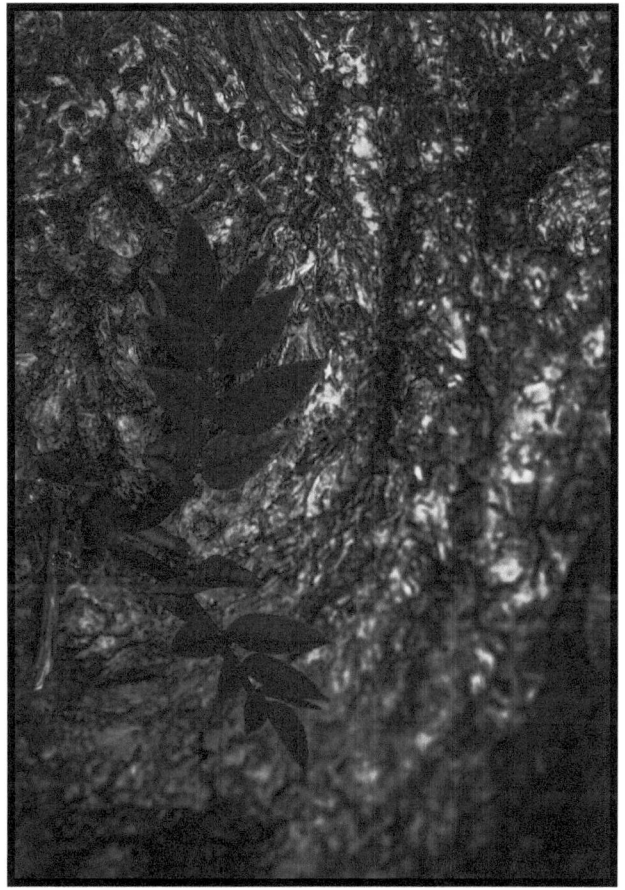

Every year again

the old tree in the garden

gives deep rooted shade

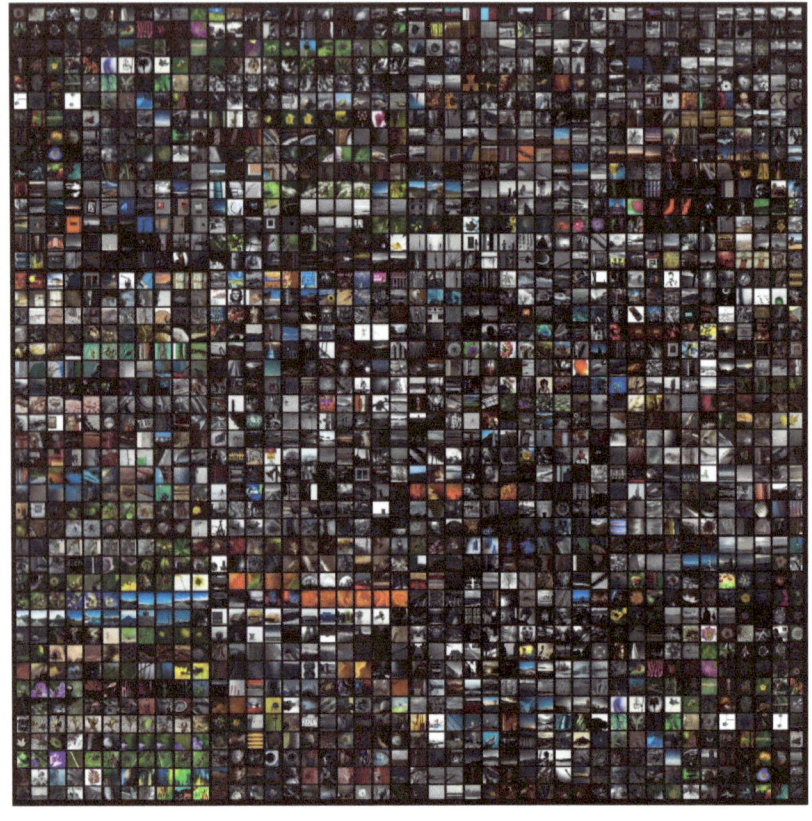

www.nochrisis.blog

www.ingramcontent.com/pod-product-compliance
Lightning Source LLC
Chambersburg PA
CBHW040233220526
45473CB00001B/227